AMAZING ANIMALS
OCELOTS

BY MARI BOLTE

CREATIVE EDUCATION • CREATIVE PAPERBACKS

Published by Creative Education and Creative Paperbacks
P.O. Box 227, Mankato, Minnesota 56002
Creative Education and Creative Paperbacks
are imprints of The Creative Company
www.thecreativecompany.us

Design by The Design Lab
Art direction by Graham Morgan
Edited by Jill Kalz

Images by flickr/Biodiversity Heritage Library, 7, 8; Getty Images/Alejandro Miranda / 500px, 10, diegograndi, 14, eli77, 9, Joe McDonald, 18, Leonardo Prest Mercon Ro, 21, Matteo Bruni, 13; Shutterstock/Saad315, cover, 1; Unsplash/Daley van de Sande, 6; Wikimedia Commons/Ana_Cotta, 17, Lewis Clarke, 5, Mark Dumon, 16, Tony Hisgett, 2, unknown, 22–23

Copyright © 2025 Creative Education, Creative Paperbacks
International copyright reserved in all countries.
No part of this book may be reproduced in any form
without written permission from the publisher.

Library of Congress Cataloging-in-Publication Data
Names: Bolte, Mari, author.
Title: Ocelots / by Mari Bolte.
Description: Mankato, Minnesota : Creative Education and Creative Paperbacks, [2025] | Series: Amazing animals | Includes bibliographical references and index. | Audience: Ages 6–9 | Audience: Grades 2–3 | Summary: "Discover the master-of-camouflage ocelot! Explore the wild cat's anatomy, diet, habitat, and life cycle. Captions, on-page definitions, an Aztec animal story, additional resources, and an index support elementary-aged kids"—Provided by publisher.
Identifiers: LCCN 2024011025 (print) | LCCN 2024011026 (ebook) | ISBN 9798889892434 (library binding) | ISBN 9781682776094 (paperback) | ISBN 9798889893547 (ebook)
Subjects: LCSH: Ocelot—Juvenile literature.
Classification: LCC QL737.C23 B6463 2025 (print) | LCC QL737.C23 (ebook) | DDC 599.75/2—dc23/eng/20240405
LC record available at https://lccn.loc.gov/2024011025
LC ebook record available at https://lccn.loc.gov/2024011026

Printed in China

Table of Contents

Here, Kitty, Kitty	4
A Warm Home	8
Meat Eaters	10
Calling All Cats	12
Cute Kittens	14
Looking Ahead	18
An Ocelot Tale	22
Read More	24
Websites	24
Index	24

Ocelots are small wild cats with spotted fur. They live mostly in the forests of Central and South America. They weigh about 30 pounds (14 kilograms). Not including their tails, they can grow up to 3 feet (0.9 meter) long.

An ocelot feels changes in its surroundings through the long whiskers on its face.

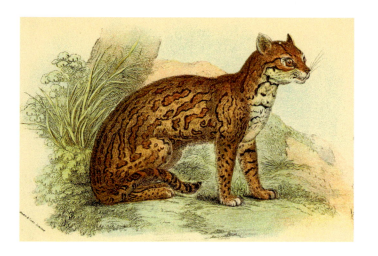

Ocelots'
golden fur is covered with two-tone spots called rosettes. Their bellies are whitish. Their small round ears are black with a white spot in the middle. Large round eyes help the cats see in the dark.

Rounded ears help ocelots hear sounds in front of them.

An ocelot's tail can be up to 18 inches (46 centimeters) long.

Most ocelots live in warm, wet places. They need thick leafy plants and bushes in which to hide. Their spotted fur is good camouflage. During the day, ocelots sleep in trees or inside dens. At night, they hunt for food.

camouflage the ability to blend in with the surroundings

Ocelots creep, jump, swim, and climb trees to get food. They eat mostly mice and rats. They also eat fish, lizards, and birds. Young deer and small pigs called peccaries may be part of an ocelot's diet, too.

Ocelots are meat eaters that hunt mostly at night.

Ocelot urine is oil-based. It does not wash away when it rains.

Ocelots usually live alone. Protecting their territory is important. Males mark it with urine and feces. The smell tells other males to stay away. A male's territory may overlap the space of four or five females.

feces bodily waste

territory an area of land claimed by an animal

OCELOTS

Ocelots breed year-round. Females give birth to up to three kittens at a time. Each kitten weighs about half a pound (227 grams). Kittens are born with spots, but their coats are gray, not gold.

A mother ocelot moves her kitten by carrying it in her mouth.

An ocelot kitten's eyes are closed for the first two weeks. After three weeks, kittens begin to walk and play. Their mother teaches them how to hunt and eat meat.

In the wild, ocelots usually live about 12 years.

Border fences break up ocelot territories, making it hard for the animals to find mates.

OCELOTS

Ocelots face danger from other animals. Jaguars, wild dogs, and wild hogs hunt them. People are dangerous, too. They turn ocelot **habitats** into farms and roads. This leaves the cats with no place to live.

habitats the natural homes or environment of a plant or animal

The ocelot's spotted fur was once in high demand for fashionable coats.

Ocelots once lived in large numbers in the United States. Today, only about 100 live in the wild. Zoos are breeding **captive** and wild ocelots. They plan to release the kittens into the wild and grow the ocelots' numbers again.

captive kept by humans

21

OCELOTS

An Ocelot Tale

The most

fearsome Aztec warriors were called the ocelot warriors. They wore ocelot or jaguar skins, including the head. They worshipped the god Tezcatlipoca. His name means "smoking mirror." The god could turn himself into a spotted cat. He also carried a mirror made from a black stone called obsidian. In his honor, the ocelot warriors made their weapons out of that stone.

Read More

Hansen, Grace. *Ocelot*. Minneapolis: Abdo Kids Jumbo, 2023.

Sommer, Nathan. *Harpy Eagle vs. Ocelot*. Minneapolis: Bellwether Media, 2024.

Websites

Carolina Tiger Rescue: Ocelots
https://carolinatigerrescue.org/kids-ocelots
Learn about ocelot features, behavior, and habitats.

National Geographic Kids: Ocelot
https://kids.nationalgeographic.com/animals/mammals/facts/ocelot
View photos and a map about ocelots.

Note: Every effort has been made to ensure that the websites listed above are suitable for children, that they have educational value, and that they contain no inappropriate material. However, because of the nature of the Internet, it is impossible to guarantee that these sites will remain active indefinitely or that their contents will not be altered.

Index

camouflage, 8
dangers, 19
ears, 7
eyes, 7, 16
food, 8, 11, 16
fur, 4, 7, 8, 15, 20
homes, 4, 8, 12, 19
hunting, 8, 11, 16
kittens, 15, 16, 20
sizes, 4, 15
tails, 4, 8
territories, 12, 19